Taking Your Camera to EGYPT

Ted Park

STECK-VAUGHN
ELEMENTARY · SECONDARY · ADULT · LIBRARY

A Harcourt Company

www.steck-vaughn.com

Photo acknowledgments
Cover ©Peter A. Davis/FPG International; p.1 ©Bettmann/CORBIS; pp.3a, 3b ©Cass Sandak;
p.3c ©Richard T. Nowitz/CORBIS; p.3d ©Nik Wheeler/CORBIS; p.4 ©Bettmann/CORBIS; p.5
©Cass Sandak; p.8 ©Dean Conger/CORBIS; p.9 ©Cass Sandak; p.11a ©Charles & Josette
Lenars/CORBIS; p.11b ©Nik Wheeler/CORBIS; pp.12, 13 ©Cass Sandak; p.15a ©O'Brien,
Fergus/FPG International; p.15b ©Nik Wheeler/CORBIS; p.16 ©The Purcell Team/CORBIS;
p.17 ©Charles & Josette Lenars/CORBIS; p.20 ©Marc Garanger/CORBIS; p.21 ©Cass Sandak;
p.23 ©Jeffrey L. Rotman/CORBIS; p.24 ©Richard T. Nowitz/CORBIS; p.25 ©Mike
Malyszko/FPG International; p.27 ©Les Pickett;Papolio/CORBIS; pp.28a, 28b ©Charles &
Josette Lenars/CORBIS; p.29a ©Cass Sandak; p.29b©The Purcell Team/CORBIS.

All statistics in the Quick Facts section come from *The New York Times Almanac* (2000)
and *The World Almanac* (2000).

Contents

This Is Egypt 4

The Place 6

Cairo 10

Places to Visit 12

The People 14

Life in Egypt 16

Government and Religion 18

Earning a Living 20

School and Sports 22

Food and Holidays 24

The Future 26

Quick Facts About Egypt 28

Glossary 30

Index 32

This Is Egypt

Egypt is a large country on the northeast coast of Africa. It is one of the hottest and driest places in the world. People have been living in Egypt for more than 5,000 years. They lived in the Nile River Valley and the delta, or mouth, of the Nile. These are also the areas where most Egyptians live today.

Egypt has many interesting cities. One is Cairo. It is the largest city in Africa. Egypt's second largest city is Alexandria. It is on the Mediterranean Sea and is the country's largest port. Two famous buildings were built there in ancient times. They were a lighthouse and a library.

There are many beaches in Alexandria.

The Valley of the Kings

Egypt also has some of the oldest known temples in the world. The temples at Luxor and Karnak are famous. The Valley of the Kings, where many ancient Egyptian rulers were buried, is also well known.

This book will show you some of these places. It will also tell you much about the country of Egypt. If you know about Egypt before you take your camera there, you will enjoy your visit more.

The Place

Egypt is part of a group of countries called the Middle East. The Middle East includes countries from Iran in the northeast to Egypt in the west. Egypt is roughly a square shape. The country is three times the size of the state of New Mexico.

The Mediterranean Sea is to the north of Egypt. The Red Sea is to the east. The Sinai Peninsula is on the northeastern corner of Egypt. The Sinai is a strip of land that connects Africa and Asia. Egypt has 1,519 miles (2,450 km) of coastline. Its land borders are with Israel, Libya, and Sudan.

The Suez Canal is a waterway between the Red Sea and the Mediterranean Sea. The present canal was opened in 1869. It is about 100 miles (160 km) long. The canal is important because it is the shortest water route between Europe and Asia. As many as 50 large ships a day may use the canal. Ships pay fees that help the Egyptian economy.

 6

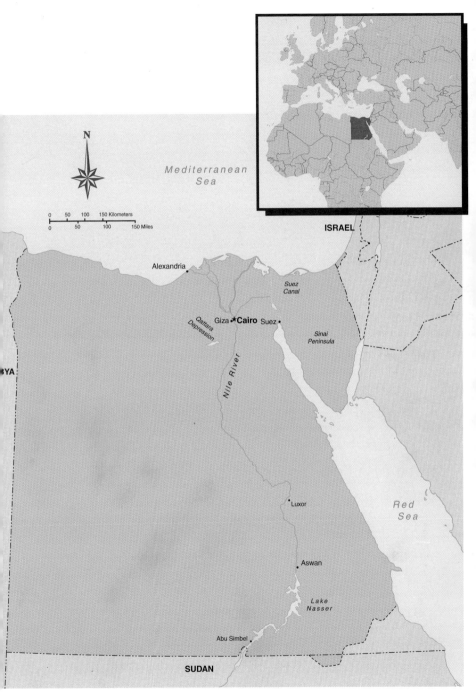

N

Mediterranean Sea

0   50   100   150 Kilometers
0   50   100   150 Miles

ISRAEL

Alexandria

Suez Canal

Qattara Depression

Giza ★**Cairo** Suez •

Sinai Peninsula

Nile River

YA

Red Sea

• Luxor

• Aswan

Lake Nasser

Abu Simbel •

SUDAN

7 📷

The Suez Canal

The Nile River flows from south to north. It is 4,145 miles (6,671 km) long. Almost a 1,000 miles (1,609 km) of the Nile flow through Egypt. The river widens at the north and fans out to form a delta.

Most of Egypt is desert. Less than 2 inches (5 cm) of rain falls each year in the desert. A hot wind, called a khamsin, blows out of the south between March and May. Sometimes it causes sandstorms. The Qattara Depression is a low area of the desert southwest of Alexandria. Parts of it are 440 feet (134 m) below sea level.

A small part of Egypt is not desert. The fertile Nile River Valley runs north to south on the eastern side of the country. It stretches for only a few miles on each side of the river. Even in the north, the total rainfall each year may be as little as 7 inches (18 cm).

In the western desert, there are a few villages. They are usually found near oases. An oasis is an area in a desert where water comes to the surface.

There are some mountains in the south and on the Sinai Peninsula.

Sailing on the Nile

Cairo

Cairo is the capital of Egypt. It grew as the center of a trade route between North Africa and the Middle East. Cairo is Egypt's center of trade and government. It also has a famous museum of Egyptian art.

Cairo is one of the world's largest and most crowded cities. About 10 million people live there. This is about one-sixth of all Egyptians. About 5,000 more people arrive in the city every week.

Although Cairo has a modern subway system, the trains are always crowded. More than 3 million riders a day use the city's bus system. Wider roads and bigger bridges have been built, but the city is always full of traffic.

Cairo is divided into the new city and the old city. New Cairo has wide streets and skyscrapers. Old Cairo is full of mosques, which are buildings in which Muslims, who follow the teachings of Mohammed, worship.

The famous pyramids near Cairo were built in ancient times.

The City of the Dead is a cemetery on the eastern side of Cairo. Many of the tombs are small buildings. As many as a half million people have moved into them and live there.

The pyramids at Giza and the stone statue of the Great Sphinx are close to Cairo. At times air pollution is so bad that they cannot be seen clearly.

Cairo is a crowded city where buildings are close together.

 # Places to Visit

Thebes was the capital of ancient Egypt. It was built on the Nile. Luxor and Karnak were built over the eastern part of Thebes. Both cities have ruins, or parts, of temples from the ancient days.

The Valley of the Kings is on the west bank of the Nile, across from Luxor. This was a hidden burial site for many of the Egyptian pharaohs, or kings. One of the most famous tombs belongs to King Tutankhamen. Some of the tombs can be visited today. Nearby is the Valley of the Queens.

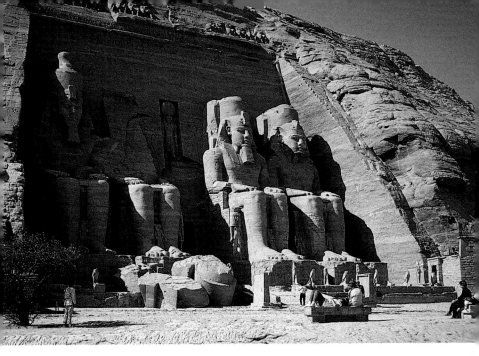

Abu Simbel now stands safely above the waters of Lake Nasser.

Aswan High Dam was finished in 1971. It is on the southern border of Egypt with Sudan. Behind the dam is a reservoir, where water is stored. It is called Lake Nasser. It is 310 miles (500 km) long and covers 2,000 sq mi (5,000 sq km). When Lake Nasser was built, it flooded much of the part of Egypt known as Nubia. A famous temple, Abu Simbel, was taken apart, stone by stone, and rebuilt on higher ground.

Queen Hatshepsut's temple is in the Valley of the Queens. She was a military leader in ancient Egypt.

The People

Egyptians are a mix of many people. Most of them are descended from the ancient Egyptians or from the Arabs who came to Egypt in the 7th century A.D. A very small number of the people are Nubians. Nubians are blacks who live in an area that borders Sudan. When the Aswan High Dam was built, much of their land was flooded.

A small number of nomads, called Bedouins, live in the desert areas. Nomads are people who move from place to place. Today the Bedouins may travel, but many have homes in towns. They also may use trucks instead of camels to carry their goods with them.

Egypt's population has doubled in the past 25 years, from 33.4 million to about 66 million people today. Half of the Egyptian people live in cities.

Arabic is the official language of Egypt. French and English are widely spoken, especially in the cities. The biggest influence in Egypt is Arabic, but particularly in the south there is an African culture.

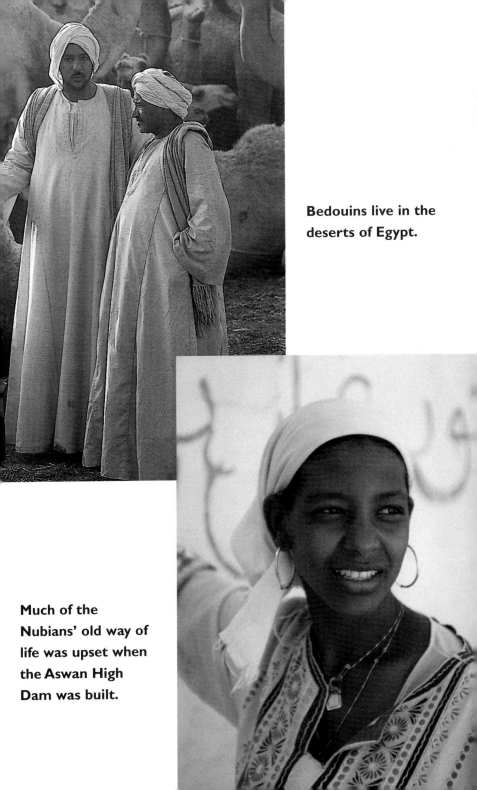

Bedouins live in the deserts of Egypt.

Much of the Nubians' old way of life was upset when the Aswan High Dam was built.

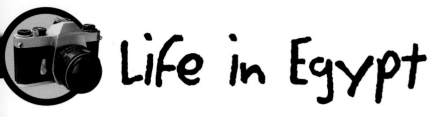

Life in Egypt

Egyptian life can be divided into three kinds. In rural areas, farming is a way of life. People who live in cities usually work in high-tech industries. Then there are Egyptians who move to cities trying to find work. Many of them cannot, and so they live in poor areas.

In Egypt, the family is important. Families often include grandparents, aunts, uncles, and cousins. They usually gather together to celebrate the most important festivals.

There are about 35 million farmers in Egypt.

At a souk Egyptians buy food and also stop to visit with friends.

Only about 4 million women in Egypt work. This is compared to about 11 million men who hold jobs. Half of all Egyptians are under 15 years of age.

Many Egyptians work in local markets, known as souks. They are also centers of business. Every village has a place where men can go to relax. But most women stay home.

Government and Religion

Egypt is one of the most important countries in the Arab world. It is a republic. This means that the president, or leader, is elected. The president is nominated by members of the People's Assembly. The citizens of Egypt then vote. The president serves for six years. Egypt also has a prime minister, who reports to the Assembly.

About nine out of ten Egyptians are Muslims. Their religion is called Islam. Muslims are very devout. For them prayer is important. Some pray in mosques. But many pray outdoors. They kneel down and face toward Mecca. All Muslims must do this. Friday is a Muslim holy day. Most businesses close. Men go to mosques to pray. Women usually gather at home to pray.

 18

Many Muslims pray five times a day.

Almost one-tenth of the Egyptian people are Coptic Christians. Coptics go back to a time in Egyptian history when most of the people were Christian. Coptic Christians hold their religious services on Sunday evenings. This is because Sunday is a working day in Egypt.

Muslims and Christians live side by side, usually in peace.

Earning a Living

Almost half of all Egyptians are farmers or herders. An Egyptian farmer is called a fellahin. Most of them live in the Nile Valley or the Delta region. Most people live along some 3 percent of the land on either side of the Nile. The land there is the most fertile and it is where Egyptians grow most of their food. However, almost all of the land has to be irrigated in order for crops to be grown. Irrigation is a way of watering plants that lets a farmer direct water to places where it is needed.

Some Egyptian farmers use waterwheels turned by animals to irrigate their crops.

Many people come from other countries each year to visit Egypt's ancient places.

Cotton, rice, corn, wheat, clover, and barley are the most important crops. The cotton industry is Egypt's largest industry. It employs almost one-third of all workers. Sugarcane is found in the south of the country, which is known as Upper Egypt.

Egypt has some natural resources. These resources are things from nature that are useful to people. They include granite, gold, oil, natural gas, iron ore, and phosphate.

Fishing is an important industry, particularly on the Red Sea. Tourism is also an important source of income.

School and Sports

In Egypt, children must go to school from ages 6 to 12. Then they go on for further schooling until they are ready for college. In the farming areas, children often do not go to school because they are needed to work. There are 13 universities in Egypt. One university in Cairo was founded in A.D. 970. But women were not allowed to attend it until 1962. One in four Egyptians is either a student or a teacher.

Because of the heat in Egypt, swimming is a popular sport. Soccer is becoming more and more important to Egyptians. There is a new stadium at Nasr City, outside of Cairo. The stadium can seat 100,000 people.

An Egyptian classroom

Food and Holidays

Most Egyptians eat rice, potatoes, bread, and vegetables. These foods are usually cooked with many kinds of spices. Egyptians may also eat meat with their meals. Meat is usually eaten with flat bread. Appetizers may include hummus, a mixture of sesame paste and chickpeas. Yogurt and a mixture of eggplant and spices are also found at many meals. The most popular dessert is very similar to rice pudding.

An Egyptian fruit stand

Most holidays center around the Islam religion. Ramadan is a period of fasting. It lasts about a month. People do not eat during the day. At night they eat a light meal. The end of Ramadan is a feast day called Id-ul-Fitr. On this day, Muslims dress in new clothes and worship at a mosque. Then they may visit relatives and eat large meals. The day ends with singing and dancing.

Flat bread is sometimes served at mealtime.

The Future

If you took your camera to Egypt, you could take photographs of many places, old and new. The country is changing, and many new things are happening there.

New cities are being built to house Egypt's large population. Health care has been made better, and people live longer than they used to. There are many young workers. People are trying to turn desert areas into farms, and Egyptians are also making computer equipment.

Like most countries, Egypt also has some problems. The country has a small water supply, and much of the land cannot be farmed. The biggest problem is Egypt's growing population.

The Egyptian people want to solve these problems. They look to the future with excitement.

Through the use of irrigation, Egyptians can bring water to desert areas.

 26

Quick Facts About
EGYPT

Capital
Cairo

Borders
Israel, Libya, Sudan

Area
386,660 square miles
(1,001,450 sq km)

Population
67.3 million

Largest cities
Cairo (6,800,000 people);
Alexandria (3,380,000 people);
Giza (3,700,000 people)

Chief crops
cotton, rice, corn, wheat, beans,
fruit, vegetables

Natural resources
crude oil, natural gas, iron ore,
phosphates, manganese

Longest river
Nile, at 4,145 miles (6,671 km)

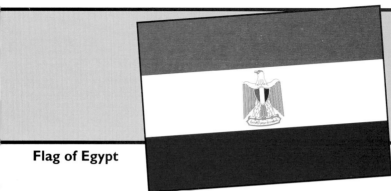

Flag of Egypt

◀ **Coastline**
1,523 miles (2,450 km)

Monetary unit
Egyptian pound

Literacy rate
51 percent of Egyptians can read and write.

Major industries
textiles, food processing, tourism

Glossary

Bedouins (BEH-duh-wuns) Nomads who live in the deserts

Cairo (KI-row) The capital of Egypt and the largest city in Africa

delta (DEL-tuh) The mouth of a river

fellahin (fel-uh-HEEN) An Egyptian farmer

irrigation (ear-ah-GAY-shun) A way of watering plants that lets farmers direct water to places were it is needed

Islam (is-LAHM) The religion begun by Mohammed

Karnak (KAR-nak) A city in southern Egypt built over part of the site of ancient Thebes

khamsin (kam-SEEN) A hot wind that blows out of the south between the months of March and May

Luxor (LUK-sar) A city in southern Egypt built on part of the site of ancient Thebes

mosques (MAHSKS) Buildings in which Muslims worship

Muslims (MUHZ-luhmz) People who follow the teachings of Mohammed

natural resources Things from nature that are useful to people

 30

nomads People who move from place to place

Nubians (NOO-bee-uhns) Blacks who live in an area of Egypt that borders Sudan

oasis (oh-AY-sus) An area in the desert where water comes to the surface

pharaoh (FEHR-oh) An ancient Egyptian king

pyramid (PIR-uh-mid) A building with four sides that come to a point at the top

Ramadan (RAHM-uh-dahn) The month during which Muslims cannot eat or drink all day

reservoir (REH-zuh-vwar) A place where water is stored

Sinai Peninsula (SI-ni puh-NIN-suh-luh) The strip of land connecting Africa and Asia

souk (SOOK) A local Egyptian market

sphinx (SFINGKS) A make-believe figure that has the head of a person and the body of a lion

Suez Canal (soo-EZ) A waterway between the Mediterranean Sea and the Red Sea. It is the shortest water route between Europe and Asia.

Thebes (THEEBZ) The capital of ancient Egypt

Tutankhamen (too-tang-KAH-mun) An ancient Egyptian king

Index

Abu Simbel 13
Africa 4, 6, 10
Alexandria 4, 8
Arabs 14
Asia 6
Aswan High Dam 14

Bedouins 14

Cairo 4, 10, 22
Christians 19
City of the Dead 11
Coptic Christians 19
crops 21

Europe 6

farming 16
fishing 21

Giza 11
Great Sphinx 11

hummus 24

Id-ul-Fitr 25
irrigation 20
Islam 18, 25

Karnak 5, 12
khamsin 8

Lake Nasser 13
Luxor 5, 12

Mecca 18
Mediterranean Sea 4, 6
Middle East 6, 10
Mohammed 10
Muslims 10, 18, 19, 25

Nile River 4, 8, 12, 20
Nile River Valley 4, 9, 20
nomads 14
Nubia 13
Nubians 14

oasis 9

pyramids 11

Qattara Depression 8

Ramadan 25
Red Sea 6, 21

Sinai Peninsula 6, 9
souks 17
Sudan 13
Suez Canal 6

Thebes 12
Tutankhamen 12

Valley of the Kings 5
Valley of the Queens 12

yogurt 24